# The Fortune-Telling Book

*The Fortune-Telling Book*
Copyright © 2006 Sweetwater Press
Produced by Cliff Road Books

ISBN-10: 1-58173-547-2
ISBN-13: 9781581735475

Book design by Miles G. Parsons

Printed in China

# The Fortune-Telling Book

SWEET
WATER
PRESS

# Maybe. Stranger things have happened.

# Shift your focus.

# It will cost you.

# Of course.

# Do it!

# Yes sirree, Bob.

# Prepare for a setback.

# Forget it.

# You're barking up the wrong tree.

# Looks promising.

# I reckon.

# Patience is needed.

# Maybe when you're older.

# After while,
# crocodile.

# Go ahead—take a walk on the wild side.

# Follow the advice
# of someone you
# trust.

# Fools rush in.

# Yes! Yes! Yes!

# Read between
# the lines.

# Don't wait
# another moment.

# Stay flexible.

# Sounds
# dangerous.

# Sleep on it.

# Play it by ear.

# Be open to
# other solutions.

# Sorry, Charlie.
# No.

# Go slowly.

# Remain flexible.

# Check out other options first.

# Opportunity knocks.

# Not on your life.

# It will blow over.

# Take a chance.

# Sounds scary.

# Ask your mom.

# Whatever.

# Tomorrow will be a better day.

# No, no, a thousand times no.

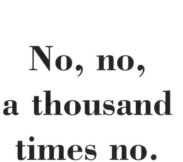

# Don't try it by yourself.

# It's doubtful.

# In the near future.

# It's a long shot.

# It would be inadvisable at this time.

# Hit 'em with your
# best shot.

# Nothing doing.

# Haste makes
# waste.

# Withstand the
# temptation.

# Thumbs down.

# No...try another plan.

# Not at this time.

# Go for it.

# Don't wait.

# Take it one step
# at a time.

# Take more time.

# It's the only way
# to go.

# Now is the time.

# There's no
# guarantee.

# Consider it a challenge.

# Don't even think about it.

# Beware.

# Seize the day.

# Can't you think of something better?

# Strike while the
# iron is hot.

# Permission granted.

# Sounds wonderful.

# Wake up and
# smell the coffee.

# Don't be
# ridiculous.

# You can do better.

# Sure thing.

# You'll never know
# if you don't try.

# Resist with all
# your might.

# It's not worth
# the trouble.

# Expect the
# unexpected.

# Delve in.

# Don't overdo it.

# Red light.

# Be reasonable.

# Use what is
# available to you.

# Not today.

# Move on.

# Roger that.

# Yellow light.

# Backpedal.

# Yes, but remember who you are.

# Put it on the
# back burner.

# Wait for a
# better offer.

# The situation is grave.

# Yes indeedy.

# Go for it.

# Beyond a doubt.

# Ask again later.

# Use caution.

# At the first opportunity.

# Retreat.

# Be more original.

# Time to punt.

# Definitely.

# You'll need more information.

# Give it all
# you've got.

# You won't be disappointed.

# Why not?

# Sounds like a
# sure bet.

# Only this once.

# Back off.

# It's a once-in-a-lifetime chance.

# Avoid it like
# the plague.

# Don't bite off
# more than you
# can chew.

# Wait.

# Later, gator.

# Leave no stone unturned.

# Keep your
# emotions out
# of it.

# Yes, but don't blame me if I'm wrong.

# It's not the answer to your problem.

# Better think
# twice.

# Do your own thing.

# There's no time like the present.

# Keep a stiff
# upper lip.

# NO! NO! NO!

# Pay attention to details.

# Hit the road,
# Jack.

# Another time maybe.

# There's no
# question about it.

When the ox is in
the ditch, it takes
unusual measures
to get it out.

# I think not.

# Seize this golden opportunity.

# It's out of your control.

# It's as good as it gets.

# Watch your step.

# Take charge.

# Walk before
# you run.

# Get more facts
# before deciding.

# Don't put all
# your eggs in
# one basket.

# Under no circumstances.

# Never.

# Indubitably.

# Nope.

# Quit while
# you're ahead.

# Why would you
# want to do that?

# I don't think so.

# Nice, but not necessary.

# Not in a million years.

# Don't hesitate.

# It won't be easy.

# Stay calm.

# Better yield.

# You're grasping
# at straws.

# Don't count your chickens before they hatch.

# In due time.

# Keep an
# open mind.

# Out of the
# question.

**No.**

# There's trouble ahead.

# Not likely.

# Get your ducks in a row first.

# Let it go.

# Avoid it at all costs.

# Yes.

# It's not your best choice.

# Nay.

# The time is right.

It's not looking good.

# Why, yes.

**Proceed with your
eyes wide open.**

# Don't bet on it.

# Be more creative.

# Sit tight.

# Think outside
# the box.

# Yeah, baby.

# It will be worth
# the trouble.

# Try something
# less obvious.

# Trust your
# intuition.

# Not today, not tomorrow, not ever.

# The early bird gets the worm.

# Thumbs up.

# The possibilities
# are endless.

# Nonsense.

# Be patient.

# Yes, no,
# maybe so.

# You'll regret it.

# You are up for the task.

# Better to wait.

# Better to be safe than sorry.

# Be more sensitive.

# Absolutely not.

# Ask your dad.

# Be my guest.

# You may wait, but time will not.

# Don't waste
# your time.

# Are you kidding?

# By all means.

# Act now or never.

# Don't bury your head in the sand.

# Pass.

# Full steam ahead.

# It's not for me to say.

# Your guess is as good as mine.

# Here we go again.

# Get out while the getting's good.

# Keep a low profile.

# Go ahead, but keep your fingers crossed.

# Face the facts.

# In a nutshell—no.

# Put first
# things first.

# Play it footloose
# and fancy-free.

# Easy does it.

# Let your conscience be your guide.

# Don't upset the apple cart.

# Let well
# enough alone.

# Nothing ventured,
# nothing gained.

# You think I have all the answers.

# Nip it in the bud.

# You'll be glad
# you did.

# There's more here than meets the eye.

# Wait and see.

# Smooth sailing ahead.

# Careful—play
# your cards right.

# You're playing
# with fire.

# That's the sixty-four thousand dollar question.

# I smell a rat.

# Take care.

# Go ahead. Take the bull by the horns.

# Throw in the towel.

# What you see is
# what you get.

That's for me to know and you to find out.

# You must be joking.

# Easy does it.

# You're only
# young once.

# Start the ball rolling.

# Let your hair down.

# Don't jump
# the gun.

# Your heart is in the right place.

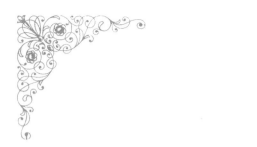

# Turn a deaf ear.

# Turn over a
# new leaf.

# It's too little, too late.

# In no uncertain
# terms—no!

# Handle it with
# kid gloves.

You have a lot
on your plate
already.

# Yes. It's just what the doctor ordered.

# Simplify your life.

It's a fool's
paradise.

# Get away from
# it all.

# You'll get more than you bargained for.

# Make hay while the sun shines.

# Don't make
# waves.

# Don't miss
# the boat.

# It's pie in the sky.

# That looks too good to be true.

# All that glitters is not gold.

# Circle the wagons.

# Speak now or forever hold your peace.

# Mum is the word.

# You can bet the house on it.

# Excellent!

# Go inch by inch,
# step by step.

# You've everything to gain and nothing to lose.

# Go ahead—live a little.

# Don't question a good thing.

# Tomorrow is only
# a day away.

# Gray skies are gonna clear up.

# Watch your back.

# Proceed if
# you must.

# I don't know
# about that.

# Are you sure that's such a great idea?

# Do you know what you're up against?

# Bide your time.

# Don't just stand there.

# All systems go.

# All things considered, I think yes.

# No, and
# that's that.

# Sure, jump on the bandwagon.

# Go ask your brother, and ask me another.

# The ball's in your court.

# You're on
# your own.

# It's an accident waiting to happen.

It's alright for
some, but not
for you.

# It's a blessing in disguise.

# Call it a day.

# Beat a hasty retreat.

# Do what
# you want.

# I'm drawing a blank.

# Hop to it.

# Proceed.

# Nobody knows
# better than you.

# Easier said
# than done.

# Enough is enough!

# Enjoy!